WORLDWIDE
CREATIVITY

This journal belongs to:

_____

and

_____

About the Author

Worldwide Creativity Mindfulness is a family-owned business born out of a desire to help children thrive by empowering them to know themselves, providing personal development activities, and helping them develop deeper connections with family while finding more joy, happiness, and gratitude.

We strongly believe that it is very important for children to grow up in a positive environment, which is why we have created these books with great care, introducing all the necessary tools for them to become grateful, confident, and open-minded.

If you find this book useful, you are more than welcome to explore our collection of mindfulness books. Also, if you would like to receive FREE self-development materials for your children and receive notifications about our new releases, please feel free to contact us.

Visit our website:
www.worldwide-creativity.com

Instagram:
https://instagram.com/worldwidecreativitypress

Facebook:
https://facebook.com/worldwidecreativitypress

A message for dad...

This journal is fun and lighthearted, asking great questions that will lead to great conversations that might otherwise be difficult to have with a teenager.

Sometimes it might not be so easy to open up, but with these carefully chosen prompts, it will be an absolutely fantastic way to record memories and encourage open communication with your children. The prompts are a great way to start the conversation and are deep enough to ask serious questions without expecting too much from them. . It switches back and forth between drawings and writing which is a good way to keep your child intrigued. Just use this journal to connect, listen and love your sweet boy, learning and affirming who he is.

With love,

Worldwide Creativity

How to use this journal

Use your imagination, remember all the good times you've had and don't overthink it, it's not a logical journal, it's a creative one. Play, be a kid, color in the images that can be colored, paste pictures where you can and have fun with your son on this wonderful journey of yours! Be passionate about what you write, share all the great memories with your son and allow yourself to make mistakes, proving to your son that mistakes happen and it's okay! Sharing this journal gives you both an opportunity to learn new things about each other and experience the emotions the other has had.

Father-Son Relationship

A father-son relationship is a beautiful and blessed one. From the birth of a son, the father plays an essential role in shaping his life. He constantly shares valuable lessons with his son and guides him in the right direction. He becomes his son's friend, guide, teacher and best companion throughout his son's childhood.

As a father, make sure you allow yourself to spend one-on-one time with your son. This time together lets your son know that he is important to you, especially if you make time for him in the midst of a busy schedule. Shared interests also become a vehicle for bonding, giving you something to talk about and do together that you both enjoy.

Focusing on your son, spending positive time together and talking about life lessons, sprinkled with a heavy dose of quiet and engaged listening, will help you develop a nurturing and meaningful relationship with your son.

So, I hope you both enjoy and engage together.

Dad and Son

This is a picture or a drawing of us

WHAT DAY IS TODAY?

Date: _____

Today is the day we give birth to this journal, the day we will always remember fondly.

Give this journal a name

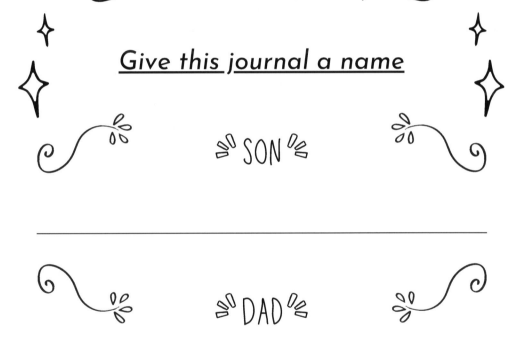

SON

DAD

 This will be your work of art. Take care of it, cherish it and enjoy it!

ALL ABOUT MY

DAD

(This is him)

My dad's name is

_____

He is _____ years old.

He does _____ at work.

He is so funny when _____

and he is happy when _____

My dad always says to me _____

_____

and he is very good at _____

_____

My favorite thing to do with my dad is

_____

My dad is the best dad ever because

_____

With love,

_____

ALL ABOUT MY
Son

(This is a selfie of him)

My son's name is

_____

He is _____ years old.

He studies at _____

He is so funny when_____

and he is happy when_____

My son always says to me_____

_____

He is very good at _____

_____

My favorite thing to do with my son is

_____

I love my son because _____

_____

With love,

_____

Personal Information

Date: _____

 We live in:

_____

_____

\\\/ **We call each other:** \\\/

_____

_____

✳ **Our eye color is:** ✳

_____

_____

☆ **Our hair color is:** ☆

_____

_____

  WRITE TOGETHER

Our
Favorite...

Date: _____

〰️ **Our favorite restaurant is:** 〰️

_____

_____

☆ **Our favorite movie is:** ☆

_____

_____

◇ **Our favorite game is:** ◇

_____

_____

Our favorite season is:

_____

 WRITE TOGETHER

Our Favorite...

Date: _____

☶ Our favorite emoji is: ☶

_____

_____

☆ Our favorite sport is: ☆

_____

_____

◇ Our favorite food is: ◇

_____

_____

〰 Our favorite place to visit is: 〰

_____

_____

WRITE TOGETHER

This is a picture or a drawing of our family

These are all of us

Their names and ages are:

_____

_____

_____

_____

Son writes

Date:

_____

DEAR DAD,

What are the three most important things in your life:

Dad writes

Date:

_____

DEAR SON,

What are the three most important things in your life:

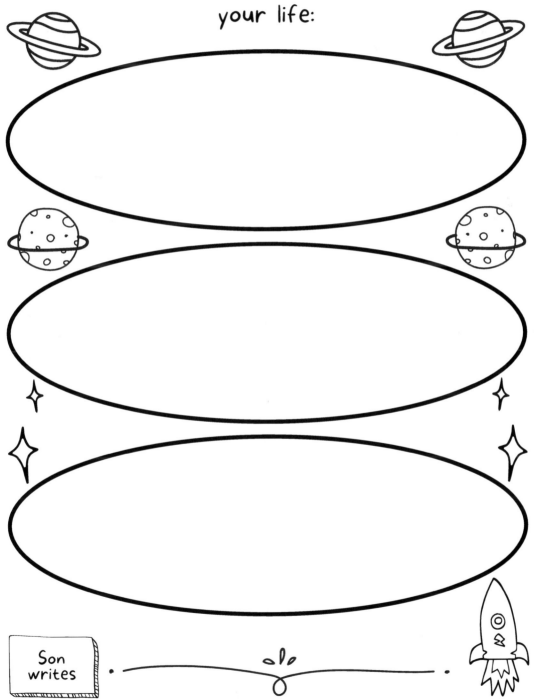

Son
writes

Date:

_____

DEAR DAD,

If you could give every person in the world one value, what would it be? What impact would this value have on society and what things could be changed for the better?

_____

_____

_____

_____

_____

_____

_____

_____

Dad writes

Date: _____

DEAR SON,

Colour the top five values that are most important to you:

Respect

Kindness ✶ Trust   Fun

Saying sorry   Honesty

Responsible

Friendship

Helping others   Faith

Creativity ✶ Happiness

Safety   Family   Patient

Being the best

Doing my best   Fairness

Popular

Being rich

School

Son writes _____

Date:

_____

Did you have pets as a child? Tell me about them.

_____

_____

_____

What is the most embarrassing thing your mother or father has ever done to you?

_____

_____

_____

What three adjectives would your grandparents use to describe you?

_____

_____

_____

Dad writes

Date:

_____

DEAR SON,

Every year, our family celebrates:

_____

_____

_____

Special things our family do together:

_____

_____

_____

Interesting facts about our family:

_____

_____

_____

Your signature

Son writes

Date:

_____

DEAR DAD,

What is the best thing your parents ever cooked?

_____

_____

_____

What did your mother or father use to tell you as a child that later turned out to be true?

_____

_____

_____

What was a favorite family tradition growing up?

_____

_____

_____

Dad writes

Date:

DEAR SON,

What skills do you have that you can use to teach others?

_____

_____

_____

If you could stop doing anything in your school day, what would it be?

_____

_____

_____

What was something you did that made you feel brave?

_____

_____

_____

Son writes

Date:

_____

DEAR DAD,

Who was your best friend in primary school? What about high school?

_____

_____

_____

What character qualities do you especially appreciate in a friend?

_____

_____

_____

Have you ever won a prize? If so, what was it for?

_____

_____

_____

 Dad writes

Date:

_____

DEAR SON,

What smell brings back a memory for you? What is the memory?

_____

_____

_____

 ## What is your favorite dessert?

_____

_____

_____

What was the worst thing you have ever eaten? Why was it so bad?

_____

_____

_____

Son writes

Date:

_____

DEAR DAD,

How did you feel about school, and what type of student were you?

_____

_____

_____

What songs have had special meaning to you over the years?

_____

_____

_____

What kind of music moves you?

_____

_____

_____

Dad writes

Date:

_____

DEAR SON,

What do you want to be when you grow up?

_____

_____

_____

What is your favorite place in the world?

_____

_____

_____

If you could invent something that would make life easier for people what would you invent?

_____

_____

_____

Son writes

Date:

_____

DEAR DAD,

Who was the hero of your childhood? What did you like most about him/her?

_____

_____

_____

What was the first album or CD you ever bought and when did you buy it?

_____

_____

_____

Were you ever on any teams or play any sports?

_____

_____

_____

Dad writes

Date:

_____

DEAR SON,

〰 **What is your biggest worry?** 〰

_____

_____

_____

If you could meet a famous person, who would
≷ it be? ≷

_____

_____

_____

If you could make one absolute rule for a day,
◇ what would it be? ◇

_____

_____

_____

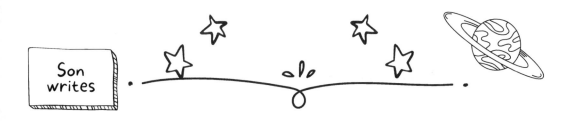

Son
writes

Date:

_____

What do you like most about your job?

_____

_____

_____

What's the best gift you've ever received? What's the best gift you've ever given?

_____

_____

_____

Is there something you've always wanted to do or experience that you haven't had a chance to yet?

_____

_____

_____

Dad writes

Date:

_____

 DEAR SON,

What would life be like if no one had a phone?

_____

_____

_____

If we had to leave today and you could only bring one thing, what would you bring?

_____

_____

_____

If you could be any age for the rest of your life, what age would you be? Why?

_____

_____

_____

 Son writes

Date:

_____

DEAR DAD,

What are you most proud of in life?

_____

_____

_____

_____

◇ What did you have as a child that kids today ◇ don't have?

_____

_____

_____

When do you feel the happiest?

_____

_____

_____

_____

Dad
writes

Date:

_____

DEAR SON,

What do you look forward to when you wake up every day?

_____

_____

_____

If only one of your toys could come alive and play with you, which one would it be?

_____

_____

_____

If you could be on a T.V. show, which one would it be?

_____

_____

_____

Son writes

Date:

_____

DEAR DAD,

✳ **What was the most difficult thing you went** ✳
through as a child?

How did you overcome it?

Dad Writes

Date:

_____

DEAR SON,

What is the most difficult thing you are going through now?

How do you overcome it? Do you need help?

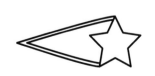

SON WRITES

Date:

_____

DEAR DAD,

What do you remember about when I was born?

How did you feel when you found out you were
going to be a father?

Dad Writes

Date:

_____

 DEAR SON,

What is something I do that makes you angry?

What is something I do that makes you happy?

  SON WRITES

Date:

_____

What are your best memories of holidays or family gatherings as a child?

What is the best family reunion or family party that you remember attending as a child?

Dad Writes

Date:

_____

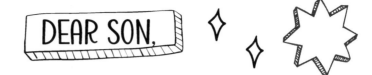 **DEAR SON,**

Son, do you know any men who inspire you to be the type of man you want to be? If so, who is that man and why?

If our whole family lived in a zoo, what kind of animals would each person be?

  SON WRITES

In what way are you most like your parents? How are you different?

What do you remember most about being a teenager? What's your best advice for me?

Dad Writes

Date:

_____

DEAR SON,

What is the funniest thing that ever happened to you?

If you could pick one meal to make for you, what would it be?

SON WRITES

Date:

_____

DEAR DAD,

What are your memories about the houses you lived in as a kid? Did you have a favorite?

What do you think was the dumbest thing you did as a child?

Dad Writes

Date:

_____

DEAR SON,

If you could travel anywhere, where would you like to go?

If you could change your name, what would you name yourself? Why?

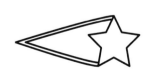

SON WRITES

 Date:

_____

 DEAR DAD,

What's one of your earliest memories?

Tell me about the three best decisions you've ever made.

 Dad Writes

Date:

_____

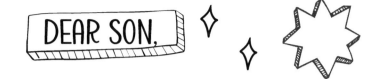

DEAR SON,

What is the worst thing that has happened to you?

What did you learn from the worst thing that has happened to you?

SON WRITES

Date:

_____

Do you believe in God?

Why or why not?

Date:

_____

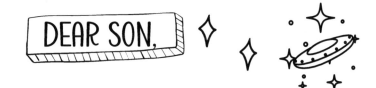

DEAR SON,

Which sense is your favorite, seeing, hearing, tasting, smelling, or feeling? Why?

What is your favorite season? Why?

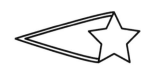  SON WRITES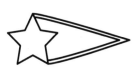

Date:

_____

DEAR DAD,

What is the best advice your dad ever gave you?

Is there anything that you wish you had asked your parents but haven't/didn't?

Dad Writes

Date:

_____

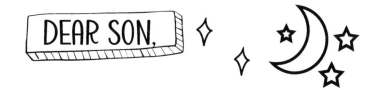
DEAR SON,

What would you do if you could do anything you wanted?

What has been the best dream you ever had?

SON WRITES

 Date:

_____

 DEAR DAD,

If you could go back to one day in your childhood, which day would that be? Why?

If you could time-travel, who would you visit and why?

  Dad Writes

Date:

_____

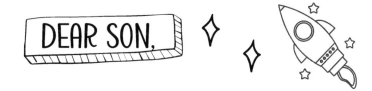

DEAR SON,

If you were to give me a nickname, what would it be? Why?

If you wanted to make everyone on the planet smile, how would you do it?

SON WRITES

 Date:

_____

 DEAR DAD,

What do you remember most about your wedding day?

What are your favorite things about my mother?
"How did you meet?"

 Dad Writes

Date:

_____

If you could change any of the rules of this world, which ones would you change?

If you could change anything about your family what would it be?

Date:

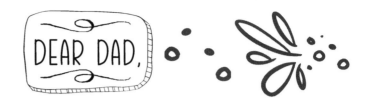

Dad, what are your hopes for me?

Dad Writes

☆ Date: ☆

_____

What do you think about my hopes for you?
Do they match your hopes? Would you like to
add or remove something?

Son writes

 Date:

_____

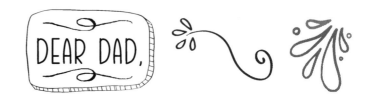

What relationship tips do you think have helped you keep your friendships and romantic relationships strong?

☆ Date: ☆
_____

What's the most important lesson you learned from me?

 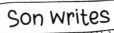

Son writes

✧ Date: ✧

_____

Was there ever a moment with me where you wished you reacted differently and how so?

 ✧

☆ Date: ☆

_____

What is your biggest complaint about me?
✧ Tell me more about that. ✧

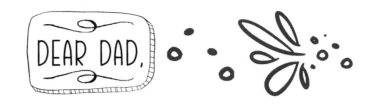

Date: _____

DEAR DAD,

How did you prepare when you found out you were going to have a son?

Dad Writes

☆ Date: ☆

_____

What is something you never thought you could tell me but maybe want to tell me now?

   Son writes

Date:

_____

How would you like to be remembered?

☆ Date: ☆

_____

What is your favorite thing about our relationship? Tell me more about that.

Son writes

Date: _____

DEAR DAD,

What's the biggest positive change you've seen in me over the years?

Dad Writes

 ☆ Date: ☆

_____

What's your biggest dream that you wish would come true?

 Son Writes

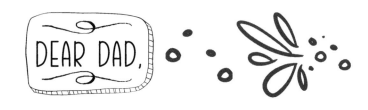

DEAR DAD,

Do you think I'll achieve my biggest dream? What advice do you have for me about my dream?

Date:

Son, where do you go for consistent encouragement to be an achiever?

Son writes

 Date:

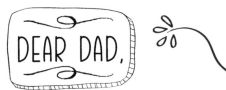 DEAR DAD,

_____

Why did you choose your career?

 Dad Writes

☆ Date: ☆
_____

If you could pick one really nice thing to do for someone, what would it be and whom would it be for?

Date:

_____

What do you admire most about your own father?

Dad Writes

☆ Date: ☆

_____

If you got to be the parent for the day, what rules would you have?

Son Writes

Date: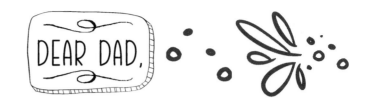

_____

Do you think my rules are good enough? If not, please explain to me why.

Dad Writes

What do you want your future to be like?

Son writes

Date:

_____

What is the first thing you say to me in the morning?

_____

What is the last thing you say to me before bed?

_____

Date:

_____

What is the first thing you say to me in the morning?

_____

What is the last thing you say to me before bed?

_____

Write Together

Date:

_____

DEAR DAD,

How do I like you to call me?

_____

How do you like to call me?

_____

Date:

_____

DEAR SON,

How do I like you to call me?

_____

How do you like to call me?

_____

Write Together

Date:

_____

If you had three wishes what would they be?

_____

_____

_____

Who do you think is the best actor/actress to play you in the movie about your life?

_____

Date:

_____

If you had three wishes what would they be?

_____

_____

_____

Who do you think is the best actor/actress to play you in the movie about your life?

_____

 Write Together

Date:

_____

Describe yourself using one word.

_____

Invent your own word. What does it mean?

_____

If you wrote a book, what would it be called?

_____

Date:

_____

Describe yourself using one word.

_____

Invent your own word. What does it mean?

_____

If you wrote a book, what would it be called?

_____

Write Together

Date: _____

How would you spend your ideal day? Try to describe in as much detail as possible what a perfect day looks like for you.

How would you spend your ideal day? Try to describe in as much detail as possible what a perfect day looks like for you.

Date:

_____

What's the hardest part about being a child?
Give me a few examples you've been through.

What is the hardest part of being a father?
Give me a few examples you've been through.

Date:

_____

When was the last time you laughed really hard and what was it about?

When was the last time you laughed really hard and what was it about?

Date:

DEAR SON,

If you had to pick a theme song to describe you, what would it be?

When was the last time you felt really lucky that something good happened to you?

What is the biggest lesson you have ever learned?

SON WRITES

Date:

_____

What are three adjectives your friends use to describe you?

1

2

3

How would people who knew you in high school describe you?

What was your first job and how did it go?

Date:

_____

 DEAR SON,

What are three things your friends would say that you are really good at?

1

2

3

If you could be someone else for a day, who would you be? Why?

What is something you are not allowed to do, that you wish you could do?

  SON WRITES

DEAR DAD,

Are there things you wish you had done differently as a father?

Do you think today's fathers have it harder or easier than you did?

What has been your favorite age so far and why?

Date: _____

What are you passionate about?

What are you thankful for?

Are you excited about your life? Is there
something you want to change?

Date:

_____

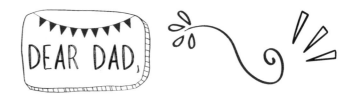

DEAR DAD,

What are the most amazing things we have done together?

1 _____

2 _____

3 _____

4 _____

Date:

_____

DEAR SON,

What are the most amazing things we have done together?

1 _____

2 _____

3 _____

4 _____

Write Together

Date:

_____

What amazing things we still have to do together?

1 _____

2 _____

3 _____

4 _____

Date:

_____

What amazing things we still have to do together?

1 _____

2 _____

3 _____

4 _____

Write Together

	SON	DAD
Favorite Color		
Favorite Instrument		
Favorite Fast Food		
Favorite Meal		
Favorite Flower		
Favorite Hobbie		
Favorite Candy		
Favorite Fruit		
Favorite Dessert		
Favorite Ice cream		
Favorite Snacks		
Favorite Drinks		
Favorite Book		
Favorite Game		

If you could design a new car that everyone would drive, what would it look like? Draw your car below.

Date: _____

If you could create a new color, what would it look like and what would you call it? Apply your new color to the images below.

The name of the color: _____

SON WRITES

Date: _____

DEAR SON,

Do you have a favorite book? What is the name of the book? Draw the cover of your favorite book below.

Your favorite book is: _____

  SON WRITES

DEAR SON,

Draw what happiness looks like for you. Use as many elements as you like and use your imagination to the full.

SON WRITES

Draw yourself in the present moment.

Draw yourself ten years in the future.

What do you think of my drawings above?
What do you think they look like?

What about my answers? Do you think
they're any good? If not, can you give some
examples?

What do you think I need to improve based
on the above?

  DAD WRITES

✧ Date: ✧

What are the three goals you have achieved so far?

Do you have other goals you want to achieve? How can I help you?

What do you think of my achievements?

What do you think of my other goals? Do you think I will achieve them?

Date: _____

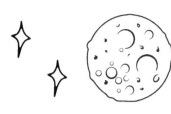

DAD, I LOVE
YOU BECAUSE
YOU ARE...

Color in each word below that represents a
quality of your father.

sympathetic

trustworthy

honest

smart

funny

hard-working

wise

supportive

loyal

patient

dedicated

strong

good listener

beautiful

humble

passionate

SON WRITES

Date:

_____

DEAR DAD,

What's something that I do that makes you proud of me?

What do you think are my best **5** qualities?

1

2

3

4

5

   DAD WRITES

Date:

DEAR DAD,

_____

What have you always wanted to ask me?

My answer

 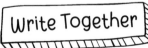 

Write Together

Date: _____  **What I love about you**

Thanks to you, I believe I can

_____

Your kind words make me feel

_____

You are a great

_____

and a wonderful

_____

I really appreciate that you taught me

_____

The most important thing for me is that you

_____

   SON WRITES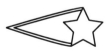

Date:

 **DEAR SON,**

What was our most beautiful trip?

_____

_____

_____

The funniest picture we have of that trip.

SON WRITES

Date:

_____

This is a picture of us being extremely happy!

Date:

_____

This is a picture of us making goofy faces.

Date:

This is a picture of us when we...

Date:

FINAL PICTURE

_____

This is a photo of us when we finished this journal.

Date: _____

Dear Son,

Ohhh, we've reached the end of this journey. What are your thoughts? Did you enjoy this journal? Are you happy with how we completed it?

What did you enjoy most?

Now that we've reached the end of this journal, what should we do next?

SON WRITES

Thank You

As a small family business, your feedback is very important to us and we will appreciate it if you could take a little time to rate it on Amazon. This will be very helpful for us, the creators of the book, as well as for other customers to analyze the quality of the product.

We really hope you enjoy our work and find it really useful, fun, and easy for you and your son, and helps you to connect with each other and to strengthen your relationship.

We create our books with lots of love, but mistakes can always happen. If there are any issues with your book such as faulty bindings or printing errors, please contact the platform you purchased to obtain a replacement.

contact@worldwide-creativity.com

WORLDWIDE
CREATIVITY

Our Growth Mindset Collection Books for kids

The bond between a mother and her son often grows out of just spending time together. A boy, who is loved and cared for by his mom, turns into a confident and strong man. This journal helps you to create strong bonds between you and your son through playful challenges, thoughtful prompts, and awesome activities.

www.worldwide-creativity.com

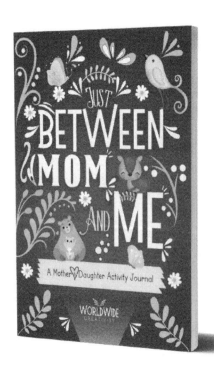

For a girl, her first role model, first best friend, and first everything is her mother. And for a mother, the daughter is a reflection. This journal helps you to create strong bonds between mother and daughter through playful challenges, thoughtful prompts, and awesome activities.

This unique activity book helps young boys train their brains, increase confidence, develop coping skills, and handle tough situations. They'll learn to feel proud of who they are as they explore their intelligence, kindness, courage, and creativity. It is also designed to help boys explore what it means to be successful, brave, and confident.

www.worldwide-creativity.com

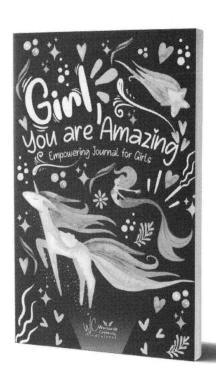

With **50** + daily activities, affirmations and lessons, girls can build up their self-esteem and transform their sense of self! The mindfulness activities encourage girls to think beyond social conventions and inspire conversations with adults about what it really means to be confident, brave, and beautiful.

Let's Connect

Can't wait to see you on **Instagram**

Instagram https://www.instagram.com/worldwidecreativitypress/

Qr-code

Can't wait to see you on **Facebook**

Facebook https://www.facebook.com/worldwidecreativitypress/

Qr-code

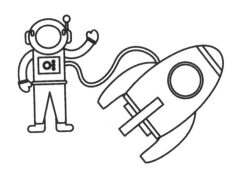

Visit our **Website**

Website https://worldwide-creativity.com/

Qr-code

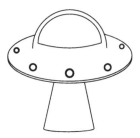

Made in United States
Troutdale, OR
11/24/2024